I SAW THE DEVIL

WRITTEN BY: BRENDON THUTSO
2021

Preface

I recently visited a mental health institution, and the stories that I heard were mesmerizing. Oftentimes, people think that someone admitted to a mental health institution is "crazy". I can confirm that the narrative is false. Those people have a story to tell, they have the experience to share, and they have battles to fight just like everyone else. We are all fighting battles, and sometimes we get overwhelmed and that can negatively impact our mental state. This visit taught me that **for every challenge we encounter, there is an opportunity to grow.**

I had the honor to talk to one admitted patient. He mentioned that his mental illness was mainly caused by drug abuse. He went through a rough time in his life when he couldn't get jobs even if he had the education to qualify for them. He said he was stressed and so he tried to find comfort in drugs and alcohol. As a result, he experienced some changes in his brain activities, and his mental health was negatively impacted. Amid all that he had been through he was still hopeful. He told me that he was hopeful that he was going to conquer his mental health illness.

 This four-part book is a journey that explores mental health and emotional issues that we all go through in our day-to-day lives. It touches on sectors like self-hate, self-love, depression, suicidal thoughts, anxiety, loneliness, self-harm, self-awareness, and fear.

Mental health is very delicate, and a large part of the world's population faces at least one mental health issue in their lifetime. We all face problems and fight battles every day and we are susceptible to mental health illnesses and emotional issues. This book serves as a guide to let you know that you are not alone and to remind you that you embody something greater than the picture that the world has drawn. I wrote this book with hopes that it will help someone to realize that we all have problems, and these problems are part of the journey that will lead us to paradise. Enjoy!

NOTE FROM THE AUTHOR:

This book is dedicated to anyone who has dealt with issues like self-hate, self-doubt, anxiety, loneliness, suicidal thoughts, depression, stress, fear, among other mental health and emotional issues. The first section of the book explores and expresses a period in my life when I felt like I couldn't get through life. We all go through rough patches in life and we feel like giving it all up. Going through tribulations feels like walking a journey through hell. The second part of the book explores how self-love and self-assurance are a road to discovering your heaven. I specifically wrote this section of the book to uplift anyone who feels like life has given up on them. We all go through a lot but we also have a lot to live for and we embody greatness.

The third and fourth sections of this book contain self-love and life principles. We all need a reason to wake up every day. This section has daily motivations, pieces of advice, and declarations that will brighten up your day.

I hope and believe that this book will be a guide that helps everyone realize that we were never promised a problem-free life but we are far greater than all the problems we face. I hope that this book empowers you and reminds you that you are powerful and that you have a great purpose to live for.

Lots of love,

B.T.

TABLE OF CONTENTS

INTRODUCTION

"Welcome to hell, we've been waiting for you", asserted a fanged old man with three eyes, a long tail, and horns. "I am the devil and it's a pleasure to finally meet you". Contrary to popular belief, the devil was short in height and hell was not as hot as Africa, it was worse. "Get yourself comfortable little sinner, we are about to make some barbeque". Exclaimed the old man. The fire was already blazing but there was no meat in sight. That's when I knew I wasn't going to be **at** the barbeque — rather I was going to be **on** the barbeque. I started running but my feet were not moving. The old man grappled me and threw me in the fire. I was roasted until I was ripe. — lol, I'm just joking, that was all part of my wild imagination.

As I grow up, I realize that the devil is someone or something right here on earth, not just a hungry old man in hell with horns, a tail, and three eyes. **Anything that blocks your road to progress is the devil.** Anything and anyone who disrupts your state of well-being **is the devil**. If you are blocking your road to progress, **you are the devil.**

We are each our own devils and angels. We hold the keys to our own perishing and our own salvation. We have the choice to curse the darkness or to light a candle. Tormenting yourself and focusing on the worst things makes you your worst enemy, it makes you the devil.

I recall a period in my life when I gave a f*ck about everyone's negative opinions about me. I would stay up all night overthinking and trying to change myself. I lost myself and I lost my identity. I looked in the mirror and I saw the devil. I allowed the world's opinions to make me hate myself. I allowed that energy into my space and I became my worst enemy. But all that changed when I started discovering the art of loving myself and unlearning the world's standards of who I should be.

*　　*　　*

We are living in a world where people set standards on how we should look, how we should be, who we should be, and how we should live. Trying to meet all these standards drives everyone to self-hate, self-harm, depression, anxiety, stress, loneliness, and fear. We look at magazines and the people termed as the standards of beauty are nothing like us and we lose ourselves because we can't meet those standards. We fail to realize that nobody is perfect and we can't always get what we want.

*   *   *

We are not going to experience life and feel like everything is perfect. We all face problems. Amid all the challenges in life, it is delicate to prioritize your mental health and treat yourself right. Mental health destruction is like a journey through hell. Avoid anything that blocks your road to progress. Know yourself and what you stand for. Realize that you are part of something way bigger than the frame the world tries to fit us in.

*   *   *

REMEMBER THESE WORDS:

"As I grow up, I realize that the devil is someone or something right here on earth, not just a man in hell with horns, a tail, and three eyes. Anything that blocks your road to progress is the devil. Anything and anyone who disrupts your state of well-being is the devil. If you have toxic friends in your circle who always see the worst in you, depress you, demean your self-esteem, cause you to hate yourself, make you feel like you are not good enough, and disrupt your mental state, they are the devil. If you have traits and vices that affect

your well-being and mental state, those are the devil. And if you are blocking

your own road to progress, you are the devil."

*   *   *

The title **I saw the devil** signifies repossessing the power stolen by the

man in the looking glass who constantly tells us that we are not worth it.

I wrote this book to guide everyone in this journey of self-discovery and

to inspire and encourage anyone who feels uninspired and discouraged.

*   *   *

I SAW THE DEVIL

When I was young I was sure of everything. I was always sure that one day I'd be a doctor, a president and I'd make the whole world happy. I always aspired to be a grown-up because I thought being grown-up means that one has it all figured out. But as I grow up I realize that life has both days and nights. Now and then, I've been overwhelmed by thoughts. I overthink everything, I stress about every task that I've failed and every goal that I haven't accomplished. I also feel like I don't have anything figured out. I stay up all night overthinking and overstressing myself. I wake up in disdain feeling like the future is bleak. I feel like a failure sometimes. I get furious at myself when things don't go my way and I end up hating myself. I look in the mirror sometimes and I barely can recognize myself. I sometimes choose to make this world a living hell for myself. I sometimes don't realize that I have a great purpose to live for and I walk through the corridors of a hell that I create. I torment myself and become my worst enemy. I sometimes open my mouth to pray but I don't even know where to start. All these emotions feel like a journey through hell. Self-love is a journey that I fail to embark on sometimes.

This section explores moments when I hate myself more and when I don't

realize the significance of the art of loving myself. The following poems best

embody this rollercoaster of my emotions:

Darkness

I closed my eyes and tried to be less awake.

I covered my ears and hoped to be less alert.

I cleared my mind to be less aware.

I held my breath and I could barely inhale.

I swallowed a knife so that I could be more abate.

I saw forms of darkness converging even with my eyes bolt.

I still heard the sound of breaking glasses with my stone-deaf ears.

I smelt and felt the fire blazing and burning my abode.

I contemplated opening my eyes, hoping it was just a nightmare.

The dark visions intensified and amplified and my eyes were wide open.

I tried to scream, but the knife sunk deep into my larynx.

I saw the darkest shadow and it was inkier than midnight.

I saw horns that were sharper than the obsidian.

I saw a tail that was longer than medusa.

I tried to take a closer look behind the shadow,

It vanished into the thick darkness.

I heard voices screaming my name.

And so I grabbed my fears and my tears.

And I dodged the sound of the voices.

The voices

I heard voices screaming my name.

They were chanting slogans of loathe and destruction.

They were growling and granting towards me.

They were voicing their diabolical opinions and words of unrest.

I tried to be vigilant but I was petrified and infused with twitchiness.

The noise intensified and vibrated deep into my soul.

I closed my ears hoping that I'd be zen.

I coiled myself with hopes that the vile words wouldn't break my bones.

I perpetuated to be silent, hoping that the noise would leave me alone.

But it persisted to tear me apart and suck up my sanity.

I ran to the east but I stepped on thorns.

I ran towards the door but it was closed.

I ran to the north but I saw eye-goggling shadows.

I ran till my feet festered.

But the vibrations of the malicious voices kept intensifying.

They were getting closer and they were ready to end me.

My ears were bleeding and I knew I was breathing my last breath.

My blood ran cold and I rested my exanimate body.

With hopes that I'd wake up in the arms of the creator.

Hell

As the world rotated on its axis, I saw a fiery furnace.

It was a concoction of fulminations and explosives.

It blazed with vigor and malevolence.

In hindsight, it permeated with all the colors of menace.

It smelt of nitroglycerine and chlorine trifluoride.

It dried all the oceans and seas.

It was a concoction of bolts of lightning and fire.

It was specifically designed to punitively torment me.

I danced to the bitter tune of the fire.

The time halted, I was roasted and incinerated.

The demons threw in more firewood and the fire roared.

The flames tormented me and I yearned for a droplet of water.

I prayed with hopes that the floodgates of heaven would let me in.

But that road had been clouded by my legion of sin.

I watched my bones turn into charcoal and my flesh to ash,

And my foe rejoiced as I turned up my toe.

Mirror

I looked at the mirror and I saw the devil.

He was very sad and he was soaked in blood.

He looked at me with his vile eyes and he shed a flood.

He reminded me of how unpleasant I was to look at.

He reminded me of all the times he slit my wrist.

He rejoiced at seeing me cry a river with him.

He threw blocks of salt in my wounds.

He told me he hated me more than death.

He jogged my memory of how far I was from heaven.

He jubilated knowing that he had dragged me to hell.

I sobbed but I never felt better.

I felt sorry for myself but it only hurt me.

I channeled the giant in me and I rekindled my strength.

 I threw a boulder in the core of the looking glass.

I watched the broken glass pieces falling.

I saw the devil screaming and passing into oblivion.

I was unbound from his chains and I was free.

I rejoiced with hopes that he had pushed up daisies.

PART II

I SAW HEAVEN

We are all walking this journey of life with hopes that we will reach heaven someday. We all yearn to be in a place of ultimate happiness, a place where there is no sorrow and crying. But sometimes it feels like such a place is far far away from where we are. When I was young I was always told that I had to die first and then my spirit would ascend to heaven where I would finally get the happiness and peace that I yearn for.

As I grow up, I begin to believe that heaven is also a part of our state of mind. Meaning that **when you master the art of loving yourself and be content with your life, you discover your heaven — A place of sanity, satisfaction, and love.** Our minds are very powerful. We have the power to make this earth a living hell or to live a heaven on earth. Of course, we were never promised a problem-free life. But that should never stop us from experiencing a heaven on earth. Amid everything that happens under the sun, you can attain ultimate happiness and you can love and accept yourself unconditionally. You don't have to be perfect to

experience an unexampled level of happiness.

This section of the book explores moments in my life when I love myself

more and when I comprehend the significance of loving myself. I always

try to make it my ambition to embrace everything that I am and to not

care about what others think of me. That feeling is a heaven that I love

visiting often. The following poems embody a heaven that I've been to:

Good place

I have mastered the art of loving myself.

I have embraced the lessons in all my mistakes.

I have mastered the creativity contained in each day.

I have seen the beauty that is contained within me.

I have understood the power and forces that I embody.

I have realized that I only live once.

I am the best person that I ever wanted to sleep next to.

I am the best friend I have always wanted to laugh with.

I am the lover that I have always wanted to love.

I've always been the lost one I was searching for.

And I have realized that everything I need is within me.

I am the truth that I've been yearning to hear.

I see the light at the end of the tunnel.

I stand and operate from the realm of divinity.

I calm violent storms and they are beneath my nobility.

I walk on the soil of the islands of the blessed.

I dwell in a state of quietude.

I am in a good place.

Anything is possible

You only fail when you don't try.

It takes laying your first brick to build a mansion.

A journey of a thousand miles begins with a single step.

It takes seven whole days to make one week.

The great Rome itself was once just a foundation.

The most significant part of success is the journey leading to success.

Never give up!

Best believe by hard work, anything is possible.

We were never promised a problem-free life.

We kick rocks, leap, then we step on thorns.

Only those who dare to leap again reach paradise.

It took Mr. Edison a thousand trials to make the first bulb.

He could have stopped trying, cried, and felt sorry for himself.

It takes the earth 24 hours to rotate on its axis.

But the earth has never halted in the first hour.

Only a loser stops trying to win.

Because by perseverance anything is possible.

I AM

I am a winner and I am a conqueror.

The fire from the hades freezes at my decree.

When I wage war, the grotesque monsters flee.

I've walked the valley of the damned, and still, I do not fear.

Because I am who I am and nothing can drag me down.

I know I am a crowned head.

I feel and I know my strength.

I hold extramundane weapons.

I know and fear no evil.

I never flinch when the devil aims at me.

Because I am who I am and nothing can drag me down.

I understand that I am not always right.

But everything I declare comes to life.

I dream of mountains and boulders moving as I prescribe.

I do the best I can, and that's nothing close to perfection.

I always hope for brighter days.

I am who I am and nothing can drag me down.

Imperfect

I am not perfect.

Sometimes I stumble and fall,

But I never stay down too long.

Sometimes I preach words,

But I'll never practice them.

Sometimes I pretend to be strong,

Then I criticize you for being weak.

Sometimes I act like I know better,

Then I turn around and do the worst.

I wipe my friend's tears away,

Then I turn around and sob a flood.

I tolerate everyone's stories,

But deep down I want them to shut up,

So that I can listen to the melodies in my head.

I am imperfect.

I wish I was young

I wish I was young!

I never used to think about a lot of things.

I never used to stress about a ton of sins.

I never used to worry about anything.

Whenever I smiled it was genuine.

Whenever I laughed it was real.

Whenever I cried, I meant to.

I never tried to convince myself that I was fine.

I never doubted that I loved myself at any point.

I never contemplated believing in myself.

I always believed that I'd someday be the greatest human.

I enjoyed my company and I was never irritated by myself.

I loved and never judged my face at any point.

I wonder why I can't look at myself in the mirror now.

I don't understand why I can't stand myself anymore.

It's a shame that I can never turn the hands of time.

If I could, I would be young again.

PRINCIPLES OF SELF LOVE

Don't you sometimes wish you could run away from all the things inside your head? I wish I could run away and hide from everything inside my head. All the voices of self-hate, doubt, criticism, and anxiety punitively torment me sometimes. I haven't fully mastered the art of loving who I am and what I look like. Every day for me is an opportunity to learn how to hate myself less. Being in a world that has expectations and standards on how I should look, how I should feel, how I should be and who I should be, it is often difficult to love myself. I find myself despising everything I am and everything I stand for, just so I can impress everyone. I sometimes listen to everything that everybody has to say about me. In the past, it was inevitable to be hurt by everyone's opinion about me. Their words would cut deeper than the obsidian. I gave the devils of the world the power to dictate how I felt about myself and I became my own enemy. Every time I looked in the mirror, I saw the devil. But all that changed when I realized that people's opinions are none of my business. My business is to love and live my life. It's always important to know who you are and what you stand for in a very opinionated world. We all owe it to ourselves to learn how to love ourselves more, unlearning how to hate ourselves, understanding that we embody something greater than anything the world has ever described, and most of all to give ourselves a little grace and showing ourselves some kindness.

The following are some principles that help me love myself more, hate myself less, and give myself a little grace:

BE YOURSELF

You can never fail at being yourself. Oftentimes, we try to live our lives based on other people's terms while neglecting our own standards. Many people have lost their identities, morals, and values trying to impress people who don't even like them. Being yourself in a world where you can be anyone, is the greatest achievement. Never allow anybody to set a pace and time for you to be yourself. If somebody has never walked a mile in your shoes, they should never have the audacity to tell you who you are. The same people that you let determine who you are, have never felt your headaches, heartaches, and pain. Live your life the way you want and be yourself because you can never go wrong when you are yourself. Destiny is not in a rush.

Being yourself does not mean you are selfish and it doesn't mean you don't care about others. Being yourself means that you like who you are and everything you stand for. It means that you are living life how you want to live it, regardless of other people's opinions. And it also means that you respect yourself.

People's opinions about you should never define you. Their opinions about you, are sorely their problem. You can't control what others think, but you can control what you think. If you live rent-free in their brains, don't allow them to live rent-free in yours. Don't allow anyone to show you how to be yourself. Nobody knows you better than you do. If you know that your morals and values are in place you have nothing to worry about. Continue to live your life the way you want. You are being judged regardless of what you do, so being yourself is the only thing that can bring you fulfillment.

Always be yourself because once you lose yourself you lose everything — your values, dreams, visions, and your purpose.

DECLARATION:

I will always be myself. I will not let other people's opinions define who I am. My values and morals are in place and that's all that matters.

LOVE YOURSELF

Self-love is your responsibility. You should be able to wake up every morning and remind yourself how much you love yourself and how much you are proud of yourself. There are some debts that you are obliged to pay, for instance; your taxes. Self-love is one of those mandatory debts that you have to pay daily. Or else one day you'll be bound by the chains of the devil and you won't break free.

It's sometimes hard to love ourselves because of our flaws, but remember that as much as we all have flaws, there is only one you for all time. I regret all the times I looked at the mirror and wished I could be somebody else because I didn't like the way I look. That was a big mistake. I should have known that I am not a mistake and I am perfect just the way I am.

We go through so much as human beings. We fight battles every day, we step on thorns, and we get hurt every other day. Investing in self-love helps us in fighting the battles of life and it helps us heal faster from our wounds.

Love yourself first, because that's who you'll be spending the rest of your life with. If you don't love yourself, you'll spend the days of your miserable life chasing after people who don't love you either. Make it an ambition to see the best in yourself and also to realize that you have been through so much and you deserve some love.

DECLARATION:

I will always love myself every day and I'll make it an ambition to see the best in myself.

BEFRIEND YOURSELF

Befriend yourself first. Get to know and understand yourself. Nobody can be a better friend to you if you have not been friendly enough to yourself. Focusing on things that you can never change about yourself only makes you your worst enemy. You can never progress if you are your enemy. Understand that you are not perfect but you are worth every good thing under the sun.

Be your priority. See the good in yourself. Love and enjoy being around yourself and be comfortable with who you are, what you are, what you feel, and what you stand for. Do everything that makes you happy, you deserve all the happiness. Sometimes the reason why you fail to befriend yourself is because of the company you keep. If you are always around a person who can't stand your guts you end up hating yourself too. There is always impartation by association. Don't be around people who make you become your worst enemy. Protect your space. Check the vibes around you. If somebody makes you your worst enemy, stay away from them. You need somebody who will love you and make you feel good.

The only way to attract such a person is by befriending yourself first, accepting that you are not perfect, and acknowledging that you are everything that you need.

DECLARATION:

I love myself, I am a great friend to myself, I will protect my space and stay away from negative energy.

KNOW YOUR WORTH

Toxic people will say things about you with malicious intent. They aim to break you down. They will try by all means to bind your brain with their words and pollute your mental space. You should always ensure the entries and exits of people in your life. Your mind should be partially permeable. It should be restrictive to anything that you deem as unfavorable. Know your worth. If respect is not being served anymore, leave the table. Never settle for less than you deserve and never settle with anybody who makes you feel anything less.

Some people have failed in their own lives and they also want you to fail and be on their level. Don't entertain them and don't allow them in your space.

The moment you allow a toxic person to walk in your mind rent-free, they will stain it and pollute it. At times, we become so good to an extent that we are easily fooled by others and they take advantage of us. Always assess who you are around. Your friends will determine the heights you reach in life. So if you are always around people who cloud you with malicious words, you can never have a clean mind. Be around people who value you and shower you with words that edify you. Don't let an insecure person project their failures on you. You are great and nobody can ever take that away from you. So know your worth.

DECLARATION:

I know my worth; I will never settle for anything less than I deserve and I will never settle with anyone who makes me feel anything less.

LIVE YOUR LIFE

YOLO (*You Only Live Once*) is a very common acronym that everyone should live by. I used to be very scared to do the things that I deemed could bring me joy. Part of the reason I was scared was that the people around me would have had a lot to say about it and partly because I was scared to break ties with people. I would neglect myself and regret it later. There is nothing as heart-pinching as having regrets over not pursuing an opportunity that you know you had a shot at.

We waste a lot of our energy trying to impress people while neglecting our happiness and lives. Don't waste your time focusing on things that don't make you happy and things you do not like about yourself. Focus on what makes you happy, focus on edifying yourself and focus on showering yourself with love because one day, you'll have the last day to reflect on the life you are living and wonder if your life was worth living. Create a life that you'll look back at one day and be filled with joy. Don't rely on anyone to make your life the masterpiece you want it to be. The only person who has the power to live your life is you. Edify yourself and reach that paradise you desire and be that happy person you yearn to be with. Whatever you do with your life, you can not make everyone happy. You are not money after all. So do not waste your energy trying to impress people. You only live once, so why not live your life the way you want.

DECLARATION:

I will not waste my energy on things that do not make me happy. I only have one life, I will live it to the fullest and make it worth living.

BE PROUD OF YOURSELF

When I was young I was discouraged from praising myself or clapping my hands because people would exclaim it as a sign of pride. But as I grow up, I feel the need to clap hands for every little thing that I accomplish and for every problem that I face. Because nothing in this life is easy and nobody has the time to give me a standing ovation because they also have their problems to battle. My advice to you is to give yourself some grace. You wake up every morning to fight battles that nobody else would be able to withstand. Be proud of yourself because that takes courage and strength. Many people are committing suicide today because they feel overburdened by their problems. And yet you are still standing and facing your problems. Superheroes do not have to wear capes or have lightning and spiderwebs coming out of their fingers. Superheroes believe in themselves, they fight battles every day and face their problems every day. You are a superhero and never think less of yourself. Clap hands for yourself because no matter how hard life's boulders hit you, you are still standing and hoping for a better day. Keep doing what you are doing. You are doing great and you are wearing shoes that would never fit on anybody else's feet. Clap hands for yourself.

DECLARATION:

I am well-pleased with myself. Life throws boulders and yet I am still standing.

GIVE YOURSELF GRACE

We stress and abuse ourselves a lot because we yearn for people's approval and people's love. We are too invested in getting validation from other people because we assume that is the ultimate road to happiness. But the truth is that nobody cares about you as much as you do. We are the ones who can love ourselves best. People's opinions about you have nothing to do with you. Taking them to heart will only result in you losing your identity. Love yourself, take your time and realize that you are good enough and you are great. You don't need a stamp from anyone to certify your greatness. You need your love and grace. Make it your ambition to soak yourself in love and to give yourself some grace. The reason why everybody on social media is posting a non-existent life is that they are all trying to get a stamp for others. They all suppress who they are so that others think they're "cool." They don't love themselves and they don't appreciate what they have. They punish and imprison themselves. Enjoy and accept your life. You are very significant and your life is not a mistake. Love yourself more and stop trying to conform to standards that you can not meet. Don't hurt yourself.

You are carrying a huge load and you are fighting and winning battles that no one in this world can ever win. Give yourself a little grace and be kind to yourself, nobody can ever walk a mile in the shoes you are wearing.

DECLARATION:

I'll make it my ambition to soak myself in love and give myself a little more grace. I do not need validation from anyone. Everything I need is within.

FALL IN LOVE WITH YOURSELF

I always thought that people had to love me or fall in love with me for me to be happy. That was my biggest mistake. You don't need people to accept you or fall in love with you, for you to be happy. You need to love yourself first and that is the only way you can be happy. You can try to impress people all you like, as long as you don't love yourself, they will never love you and you'll never be happy. Nobody can make you happy. They can excite you, make you laugh, or smile, but you are the one with the power to make yourself happy. Love yourself and accept everything about yourself. Understand that nobody is perfect. We are all on a journey in search of happiness. Self-love is the widest step you can take to be closer to your destination. Shower yourself with love and you will know what it feels like to be happy.

A woman is crying in her room because the world has told her that her body is not perfect. A man is stressed and overthinking because the world told him that he is not man enough and he is not good enough. We allow the world's opinions to dim our lights and draw us far away from happiness. Do not allow the world to make you question things that you can't change about yourself. Your love and acceptance are the only fuels you need for you to reach happiness.

Believe that you are wonderfully made and you are unexampled. Don't let people's views about you be a template of how you define yourself. Love yourself. To fall in love with yourself is the secret to finding happiness.

DECLARATION:

I will fall in love with taking care of myself, I will fall in love with the path that leads to my healing, I will fall in love with becoming the best version of myself, and I will fall in life with myself.

WORK ON YOURSELF

You are the greatest project you'll ever work on, take your time and create magic

Nobody is ever perfect. We are all projects, and every day is our opportunity to work on ourselves and to achieve our desires. We usually have anxiety because we don't have everything figured out and we assume that everybody else has everything figured out because of what we see on social media platforms. But reality is very different from social media. Nobody has it all figured out. Everybody is trying to figure things out. Nobody is sure of the future, everybody has problems. Don't let social media drive you insane. Everybody on social media portrays an image. But that's just what it is, an image. So don't be rushed, take your time and work on yourself. Don't let social media make you feel like you are too late. Nobody has the power to edify you. The power is in your hands, use it and create magic.

Nobody has the time to work on you, we are all working on ourselves too. Don't rely on someone to come with bricks so that they can build you, some people might throw the bricks at you and destroy you. Don't work at someone else's pace. We are different. We all have our paces and purposes. What someone gets might not be what you need at that time.

Be grateful that you still have the opportunity to do better. Build yourself,

invest a lot of love in yourself and cement it with faith.

DECLARATION:

Greatness is my birthright. I might not have everything figured out but I

am a work in progress and nothing can dim my light.

STOP COMPARING

Comparison is the thief of happiness

Just because others are getting accolades it doesn't mean that you are not fulfilling your intended purpose right here on earth. It doesn't make you any less human. Stop focusing on what others are doing and getting. Focus more on edifying yourself and enjoying your ride. Our journeys and purposes are different. We can never be the same. We all contribute unique aspects to the world. And that's what makes it all beautiful. When someone is shining, your light is not dimmed in any way, instead, it allows you to shine your light in your direction and look forward. The reason why some people hate people whom they don't even know is that they compare themselves to them and when they notice that they can't compare they become jealous and start spreading hate. Comparison steals joy and it makes you ungrateful and sour-hearted. So instead of comparing yourself to other people, wait for your time to come, seek your purpose, and be grateful. Destiny is never in a rush, you are. Everything falls in line when the time is right. Understand that where someone else is in life does not determine your stature in this world. The only person you should be comparing yourself with is the person that you were yesterday. Ask yourself if you are better than you were yesterday. Ask yourself if you have grown from who you were yesterday. If the answer to those questions is yes, then you are winning and you have every reason to be grateful.

DECLARATION:

I will not compare myself with anyone because I have my intended purpose. I am alive and I am better than I was yesterday. I have every reason to be grateful.

LET GO

In the bible, Lot and his family were told to flee from Sodom because a disaster was to descend on the land. While they were fleeing, Lot's wife looked back at Sodom. She couldn't let go of the life that she had lived in sodom. Since she couldn't let go, she turned into a pillar of salt. She looked back at a life that didn't serve her best interests and that led to severe consequences.

At times we don't want to let go of some things because we are too comfortable with them or because we are scared of living a life without them. It's good to hold on to something that drives you and also carters for your future. But if you are holding on to something toxic or something that you know is not best for you, it is likely to be the cause of your perishing. You have to be able to discern what to hold on to and what to let go of.

 If you don't let go of things that do not serve your needs, you burden yourself with a load that will only break your backbone and still not edifies you in any way. So if you are holding on to things ask yourself if those things will edify you in any way. And if the answer is no, then let

them go because you can't afford the cost of losing yourself over things

that do not contribute to your purpose.

DECLARATION:

I will not hold on to anything that does not serve my needs.

FACE YOUR PROBLEMS

Life can be cruel sometimes. We get overwhelmed by the problems life throws at us and because we are only human, we try to find a savior in all the wrong places. I recently visited a mental institution in Zimbabwe. I was listening to all the stories of the admitted patients. Most of them were talking about how they were faced with problems such as failure at school, being broke, or losing jobs. Since they didn't know how to deal with their problems, they started overdosing on drugs and alcohol. And the abuse of those substances played the role of destroying their mental health and that led them to mental institutions. The moral in all of this is that your vices will never solve your problems, they will multiply your problems. Don't try to find a savior in substances or alcohol, they will destroy you.

You can feel sorry for yourself and intoxicate yourself all you want, but your problems will be standing right in front of you, waiting for you to face them. The longer you use your vices as a cave to hide from your problems, the more your problems give birth to more problems. You have to understand that for every problem you face, there is a solution within you. You are never given problems that you can't handle. It's never easy to face your problems but it is worth it. The more you do not deal with your problems, the more they acquire the strength to deal with you. Make it your ambition to never use your vices as a cave to hide from your problems. Understand that you embody greatness and no problem is greater than you.

DECLARATION:

I will face my problems because I am way greater than any problem that I face.

AVOID TOXICITY

Your peace of mind is delicate and it should be your number one priority.

Once you lose your peace you lose yourself and everything you stand for.

Toxicity is similar to the concept of diffusion. It moves from an area of

higher concentration to an area of lower or no concentration. So beware

of all the people and energy you allow in your space.

Toxic people do not care about how you feel and how you are, they only

care about themselves and their image. They do not care if you are hurt

in the process. They are willing to project all their insecurities and

troubles on you. I'm sure you have had an encounter with a toxic person

— the one who leaves you feeling worse off after interacting with them.

Maybe it's a manipulative family member, an acquaintance or a coworker

who can't stop complaining about every little thing. They believe they

are never wrong. They would rather sacrifice your name to save their

image. It's very hard to deal with such people because they are very

manipulative and they are willing to paint themselves as victims. The only way to avoid them is to stop playing into their reality and walking away from them.

Your peace of mind should be an aura where you feel the most comfortable and secure, it should be a haven for you. So if someone fills that aura with toxins and negative energy, stay away from them. Make it your ambition to unsubscribe to all toxicity and treat yourself right.

DECLARATION:

I will protect my peace at all costs, I will unsubscribe to all toxicity and I will treat myself right.

PART IV

PRINCIPLES OF LIFE

A lot of voices try to discourage you. The most powerful of those voices is the one that is inside you. You doubt yourself a lot and you doubt your capabilities. Once you doubt yourself you lose sight of your full potential in life.

Know who you are and what you stand for. There is a difference between **existing** and **living**. When you are existing you just continue to be alive in flight mode. But when you are living you enjoy your life, you savor every moment of life, you embrace life and you take life as it comes. It's not dying that scares me, it's dying when I haven't lived my life.

Live your life, take care of your business and embrace who you are. No matter how tough life may be, it's always delicate to know who you are and to embrace life as it comes. We were never promised a life without problems. Everyone faces problems in life, the greatest achievement is being able to live your life amid all trials and tribulations. Living life is acknowledging the existence of your problems and dealing with them, existing is acting like your problems don't exist.

Only those who dare to move forward after stepping on thorns can live their life to the fullest. You can do anything that you put your mind to. The simple principle of life is that life responds by corresponding: your life becomes what you decide it to be. Life changes as much as you want it to. Your efforts in life should be supplementary with your goals.

The following are some of the principles I live by to edify myself daily and quench any thoughts of self-doubt and anxiety:

EMBRACE YOUR PROBLEMS

Sometimes the only way to solve a problem is to first acknowledge and accept that it exists. When you are experiencing a problem, you sometimes feel like the future is bleak and you will never get through it. So you ignore it hoping that the problem will just disappear. Acknowledging the existence of your problem might help you figure out the best means to get rid of your problem. It can also introduce you to your true strength.

The problems that you are experiencing are usually a detour that will lead you right where you are supposed to be. It might not feel that way when you are going through problems. You might feel like running away and hiding. But remember this; running away is super easy, facing problems makes you stronger than before. We all want to experience a life without problems and feel like everything is ok. But we were never promised a problem-free life. Embracing every problem is a wide stride towards solving them. It is important to know and understand that every problem that you face is specifically designed to teach you something. The adventure is in discovering that lesson and realizing your strength. A road without problems is inevitable. We all walk that road. We all step on thorns but only winners dare to stand up and leap again. So embrace all the problems that you face, learn a lesson from them, and realize your strength. Your problems are a part of your journey and they are meant to drive and to push you to the right destination.

DECLARATION:

I will embrace all my problems and deal with them accordingly.

SEPARATE CHAFF FROM GRAIN

The first step to getting what you want, is to get rid of what you don't.
— Zig Ziglar

After farmers have harvested grain, they have to separate it from the

unwanted chaff that surrounds it through a process commonly known as

winnowing. They separate the mixture by throwing it in the air so that

the wind blows away the inedible chaff and the edible grain gets

recovered. Winnowing is equally important when going after your goals.

To obtain what you want, you have to get rid of what you do not want.

So if you want to achieve certain goals, look for the obstacle that is

hindering you and get rid of it. If you have a toxic member in your circle,

get rid of them and remain with people who edify you.

Chuff is very light and it can be easily blown by the wind. That's exactly

how obstacles are. They are temporary and they do not have value. They

will never hold you down when you face hardships. That's why getting

rid of them is essential. On the other hand, grain is heavier and it holds

weight. And that is how things you keep around should be. They should

hold weight. They should not be moved easily by any type of force. They should be able to hold you down no matter what situation you have going on.

It's so easy to hold on to obstacles that hinder us from success. It may be our vices, doubt, fear of the unknown, bad company, and so forth. But those things can easily be blown by the wind, so holding on to them is never worth it. You have to let go of everything that is not in your favor then your blessings will overflow. If you don't let go of whatever is blocking you from seeing the light, you will always be in the darkness. It's not easy to let go of anything, but if it doesn't edify you, it is very necessary to let go.

DECLARATION:

I will get rid of any obstacle that hinders me from progressing.

INVEST YOURSELF

In physics, Newton's first law of motion states *"an object at rest stays at rest and an object in motion stays in motion in constant velocity unless acted upon by a force"*. This means that if you want to see a change, you have to invest some effort. The more effort you invest, the more the change that you observe. If you want to see a change in life you have to make sure that you are working towards it. Don't expect change if you do not invest any effort.

If you want to be something, be. You have the power to do anything, to be anything, and to have anything. It all depends on how much you want it and how much of yourself you are willing to invest. The effort you invest in life yields the exact effort that life invests in you. So to achieve your desires abundantly, you also have to invest a lot. People always want to put very little effort into their dreams, visions, and ambitions, and then they cry a river when their dreams are not fulfilled. Invest yourself in your dream. You have to invest in real skills and work for what you desire. Don't expect to build a mansion when you don't lay the bricks.

Being lazy is an unhelpful trait that will lead you nowhere. If you want to see a change you have to take some action towards it. Invest yourself, put more effort and you will see a change.

DECLARATION:

I will invest myself in life and work towards achieving my goals.

BELIEVE IN YOURSELF

Believing in yourself is a prerequisite to accomplishing your goals. If you do not believe in yourself, you can kiss your goals goodbye. You have to change your perspective of life. Stop focusing on what could go wrong and focus on what could go right. You have everything it takes to do whatever you put your mind to. You are braver than you think, more talented than you know and more capable than you can ever imagine.

Learning to believe in yourself is a wide step towards creating a life that you desire. Do not undermine the power that you possess. If you can think of something, you can do it. We restrict ourselves from following our goals sometimes because we are scared that our abilities might be insufficient. Those thoughts are the voice of the devil and they are there to destroy, steal and kill your confidence. You have the power to do anything. As long as you believe in yourself, you will find your way. The level of success that you achieve in life is a result of your belief system. So start believing in your capabilities. Conquer your doubts because they only set you back and they pull you far from achieving your goals. When you believe in yourself you break a lot of barriers. So make it your ambition to solidify your belief system and you will see that even the sky can never be your limit.

DECLARATION:

I believe in myself. I know that I have everything it takes to accomplish my goals.

JUST DO IT

Don't let dreams just be dreams. Wake up and do something about them.

They will not manifest unless you act upon their manifestation.

Everybody is always looking for shortcuts and handouts to living life. But

those do not exist. You just have to do something for yourself to see

results. The key is in remembering that you can do anything. As long as

you work towards it.

Oprah Winfrey is one of the most famous t.v presenters ever because she

dared to act upon her dreams. It did not happen overnight, she was once

fired and told that she was "unfit for television". But that did not stop her.

She still pursued and worked towards her dreams. We are sometimes

scared to do something because we are scared to fail. But in every failure,

there is a lesson that you should learn and there are corrections you will

have to implement. So regardless of the bricks that life throws at you,

just keep on doing what you have to do and achieve your goals. If it

doesn't happen instantly. Keep on daring. It will manifest at the right time and the right place. We were never promised a simple life. We all have boulders that are thrown on us, to deter us and overwhelm us. But we have the power to overcome those obstacles. We embody something greater than any problems that we face. No matter how many problems you face, you can still achieve your goals, it just depends on what you are willing to do to achieve them. So just do whatever you have to do to achieve your goals. Just do it.

DECLARATIONS:

I will do whatever I have to do to achieve my goals and all my efforts will come to fruition.

DREAM BIG AND GO BIG

No dreamer is too small and no dream is too big. Don't ever feel like your background can ever restrict you from dreaming and going after your dreams. You can accomplish your dreams and you have everything that it takes. Your dreams are valid!

Everybody who has accomplished something in life was once in your position or worse. They had dreams and they dared to follow them regardless of whatever boulder life threw at them. They believed in their dreams and went after them until their dreams manifested into their reality. Get out of your comfort zone and take action too. You have the power to transform your life into whatever you want. So don't limit yourself from working towards getting big things. Keep on dreaming and believe in your dreams and they will come to fruition.

Sometimes life doesn't give us back what we want, but what we need. Our efforts sometimes do not place us where we would want to be, but where we would need to be. So if you invest in something big and you don't automatically yield what you want, don't be discouraged, you are still at the top and your efforts will fight for you to be where you need to be. Don't give up on yourself, you are a light in this world, you have to keep shining. You are a winner until you stop trying to win. Keep on dreaming. Aim for the stars. And if you don't shoot one, at least you are amongst the stars.

DECLARATION:

I will do everything with great ambition and my efforts will place me right where I need to be.

TAKE CHANCES

In accounting, there is a concept referred to as the trial and error method. This is a process of experimenting with various means until the desired outcome is observed and by noticing errors or causes of failure. This also applies to real-life cases. You never know the outcome until you try. So instead of allowing fear to be the force that drives you. Have faith and believe in yourself. Then take your chances. And if you don't reach the goal that you wanted to reach just notice the cause of failure, eliminate it and try again. This places you a step ahead. At Least you know what not to do. So take chances, make mistakes and get messy. You only regret every chance you never took when you had a shot at it. One of the worst feelings in the world is regret. We all regret everything we think we could have done differently, everything we wish we could have said differently, and every chance we wish we had taken. Take those chances so that you never look back and regret anything. Never limit yourself. Oftentimes, self-doubt yields regret. Don't doubt yourself, take chances because things always end up the way they should be. If you feel like you can do something, do it, aim for the stars. It is better to look back and be proud of your efforts than to regret not taking a chance. So make it your ambition to take every step that is necessary towards accomplishing your goals. Because you only regret the chances you don't take.

DECLARATIONS:

I will not limit myself, I will take every step necessary towards reaching my goals.

KEEP HOLDING ON

We all wish we could experience life and feel like everything is ok. But we were never promised a problem-free life. We face problems and deal with a lot of obstacles. The future usually feels bleak when we go through problems, we feel like we can never get through them. We lose sight of the light at the end of the tunnel. We fail to realize that every problem is temporary and that better days are ahead.

The problems that you face in life are meant to teach you a lesson and to help you accomplish your intended purpose. So whenever you go through problems, don't give up. Keep holding on. Remember that the wind prevails most where it rains the most. The problems that you deal with are meant to strengthen you. You will get through them.

When you are going through a tough time, it feels like everything is against you and you may feel like you can not hang on a minute longer. Things may be very dark at the time, but always remember that the dark always comes before dawn. Some problems are a part of your journey that will eventually lead you to your destiny. It's usually hard to see through the glass when moments are foggy. But hold on to your faith and

learn the lesson hidden in your problems and dare to move forward

because that is where you are headed. Keep holding on, everything will

fall in line.

DECLARATIONS:

I will keep holding on because I can make it through anything.

NEVER GIVE UP

Thomas Edison is the first man to invent the working light bulb. It took him more than a thousand attempts before he made a working light bulb. Now imagine how the world would be if he just gave up after the first trial.

Every successful person has a similar story. They did not just wake up successful. They had to put their blood sweat and tears to get what they wanted. They faced challenges and stepped on thorns, but they never gave up. They kept their heads up high. Anything worth it doesn't come easy. You have to keep on trying until you get it right. If Thomas Edison never persisted, he would probably be one of the many forgotten people without a legacy. His efforts solidified his legacy. He worked hard and never gave up until he got it right. Never give up on your dreams. We all face problems. Only the wise realize that no problem is ever too big. Everybody that you see has their problems. But everyone's problems aren't the same. That doesn't mean others feel the intensity of problems more or less than others. Many people go through depression and anxiety because they think that problems are unsolvable. They give up and stop

trying. They forget that for every problem described, there is a solution.

It might not manifest instantly but it exists and soon enough you'll know

how to solve your problems. So never give up. You only fail when you

stop trying

DECLARATION:

I will never give up. I will keep trying until I get it right.

YOU HAVE A PURPOSE

you have a purpose in life, when you find it you will know

Whenever you wake up at 3 a.m. and stare at the ceiling overthinking and wondering what you are doing with your life or feeling lost, please just know that you are not alone. We are all in constant search of ourselves and we all wonder what this life holds for us because nobody is certain of their future. Just remember that you are supposed to be here and you are special. You are God's very own handiwork chosen and commissioned for a great purpose.

Shame on every tongue that has told you that you are worthless, don't believe them. You had a purpose even before they had an opinion. You were strategically put on earth for a special purpose, whoever doesn't believe it, has some problems to deal with. Keep your head up high. If ever you have doubts about your purpose, place your hand over your heart. Appreciate every beat you feel because someone else didnt have the opportunity to feel theirs. There is a purpose for every heartbeat you feel. You might not have discovered your purpose yet, but at the right time your purpose will unveil to you and you will be able to fulfill it. Your life is impactful, your voice is significant and your dreams count towards the betterment of this earth.

Do not underestimate your purpose and do not underestimate yourself. You are a special part of this world. And when the time comes you will know what your purpose is and you'll fulfill it. Keep holding on. The problems that you face and the sleepless nights are temporary. Continue to love yourself and to believe in yourself. You were created to fulfill a greater purpose. God does not place dice with the universe. He does not make mistakes. You are supposed to be here. Soon you will find what your purpose is and you will know when you do.

Declaration:

I am useful. I was strategically designated on this earth to fulfill that special purpose.

EMBRACE WHO YOU ARE

Embrace who you are, there can only be one you

The ability to embrace and be yourself in a world that is constantly trying to change you is the greatest achievement. You have to know yourself, love yourself, acknowledge your strengths and be aware of weaknesses. This world is always trying to erase identities. Don't lose yourself because you want to impress the world. There are people in life, who will try to make you feel miserable by condemning you. Don't help them by doing that job yourself. Embrace everything that makes you unique even if it makes everyone uncomfortable. Know your values and morals and everything else will fall in line. Nobody should have the power to define you or tell you who you are. You have that power. It's essential to know who you are, and what you stand for because if you lose yourself, you've lost everything. Do not let people project their failures and agendas on you because they are failing to find a way to live their own lives. Live and love your life. People will judge you, criticize and put you down for being different. Embrace your weirdness and remember that; When you are like everyone you are nobody. You only become somebody when you are different from everyone. Know what you stand for so that you do not fall for anything. Do not feel any need to apologize for who you are. If somebody doesn't like who you are they can fall back. You are perfect just the way you are. Stop trying to fix yourself, you are not broken, you are just different and that is your superpower. Embrace yourself, love yourself, and cherish your life.

DECLARATION:

I embrace who I am and what I stand for. I will never apologize for who I am because I am a great part of this world.

YOU HAVE SO MUCH TO LIVE FOR

Not every day is going to be perfect. We all have good and bad days. But

in all those days there is always a purpose and a lesson to be learned.

Each day is meant to edify you and equip you with the necessary tools for

you to reach your destiny. So don't take any day for granted, be grateful

that you have a chance to be who you want to be. You were specifically

designed for a special purpose. You have a lot to live for. You might not

feel that way every day because life can't go your way every day. But

there is a purpose in every breath you take.

We can't always get what we want, but we will always have what we

need. Cherish yourself and remember that you have so much to live for.

We are all human and we are nowhere near perfect. We have faults no

matter how much we try to reach perfection. Regardless, our

imperfections lead us to our designated destinations in life. That being

said, each day that we wake up, we are fulfilling our intended purposes.

So include every breath you take when you are counting your blessings.

Acknowledge the good that you have in your life, that is the foundation of all abundance. We are blessed enough to have the opportunity to fulfill our purposes. Whenever you find yourself doubting how far you can go, remember how far you have come. Always be grateful, that you are still able to transform your life however you want. Make it your ambition to cherish every breath that you take, you are making the world a better place. You are amazing and you had so much to live for.

DECLARATION:

I have so much to live for. I will not take any day for granted because there is a purpose and a lesson to be learned.

CONCLUSION

Nobody has everything figured out. We are all on a journey of self-discovery and we are all learning how to love ourselves more. The key to living life is living it to the fullest and understanding that it only happens once. Live your life and don't allow the world to make you see yourself as the devil. Hold on to your morals and values, don't conform to anyone's standards in this world, and don't allow anyone to erase your identity. If you lose yourself you lose everything in life.

* * *

Life is not easy. But it is worth living. Nobody is going to experience life and feel like everything is in place. We face problems. But amid all those problems, it is essential to remember that we are greater than the picture the world paints us to be. Keep holding on and learn the lessons contained in every problem you face.

* * *

You have the power to create the life that you want. The power is in your mouth and your hands. You have to speak and declare the life that you want, then work towards acquiring that life. It is never easy to get

something that is worth it. You have to invest yourself in it until you see
results. Not achieving goals instantly does not make you a failure. It
means that you have to keep on trying until you get it right. Only a loser
stops trying to win.

*   *   *

I pray that this book has touched your soul and opened your eyes to a
great perspective of this world. Continue to believe in yourself and know
that you were specifically designed for a great purpose. Create your own
heaven, love yourself more and always remember that you have the
power to do anything you put your mind to. Be blessed.

*   *   *

THE END

Hate

When you know that you are great,

And your morals and values are in place,

You have no reason to hate anyone.

Only a person who is defeated,

Finds art, joy, and pleasure in hate.

Only a person who loses their hope to win,

Finds a way to hate other people.

Only a failure,

Succeeds in spreading hate

Only a lazy person,

Works hard to spread hate.

It's only the heartless son of the devil,

Who finds the heart to hate.

It's only an ugly child from hell,

Who sees beauty in hate.

Hate only expresses the failures of a person who will never win.

ABOUT THE AUTHOR

Brendon Thutso is a Zimbabwean-born businessman, IT specialist, and best-selling author. His catalog sketches across many sectors, including business, romance, adventure, and mental health. All his writing is usually inspired by his experiences. He has garnered praise from media outlets for the enlightening perspective that he shares through his books. His debut book is a romance book titled 'To My Crush', published in 2019. This became Amazon's best-selling book upon release. The book is a poetry collection that the author wrote about a person they had an unquenchable crush on. His second book is a fiction book titled 'Wonders Will Never End', published early in 2020. His third book is a book titled Business Acumen. Where he guides and details the means of creating a business that yields success. The book was inspired by his successful multi-department enterprise Brendata store, which he founded in West New York in New Jersey in 2019. His fourth published book is a highly motivational self-help guide titled, 'I Saw The Devil'. In this book, he shares his perspective of life through poems and motivates readers with inspirational principles. His work is published on all book reading platforms and various world libraries.

ONE MORE THING:

Thank you very much for reading this book. If this book helped you in any way my mission is fulfilled and I am happy. Please leave a review and recommend the book to others. So that they can also learn the lessons that you learned.

MORE BOOKS BY THE AUTHOR:

amazon.com/author/brendonthutso

TAKEAWAY QUOTES :

You embody something greater than the picture that the world has
drawn
—Brendon Thutso

Problems are part of the journey that will lead us to paradise
—Brendon Thutso

Anything that blocks your road to progress is the devil.
—Brendon Thutso

Anything and anyone who disrupts your state of well-being is the devil.
—Brendon Thutso

If you are blocking your road to progress, you are the devil.
—Brendon Thutso

Everything changed when I started discovering the art of loving myself
and unlearning the world's standards of who I should be.
—Brendon Thutso

We are not going to experience life and feel like everything is perfect
—Brendon Thutso

Prioritize your mental health and treat yourself right.
—Brendon Thutso

when you master the art of loving yourself and be content with your life,
you have discovered your heaven
—Brendon Thutso

We kick rocks, leap, then we step on thorns, Only those who dare to leap
again reach paradise
—Brendon Thutso

Only a loser stops trying to win
—Brendon Thutso

Only a person who is defeated Finds art, joy, and pleasure in hate
—Brendon Thutso

It's only an ugly child from hell who sees beauty in hate
—Brendon Thutso

I sometimes wish I could run away and hide from everything inside my head.
—Brendon Thutso

Every day for me is an opportunity to learn how to hate myself less.
—Brendon Thutso

There is nothing as heart-pinching as having regrets over not pursuing an opportunity that you know you had a shot at.
—Brendon Thutso

Each day is meant to edify you and equip you with the necessary tools for you to reach your destiny
—Brendon Thutso

Learning to believe in yourself is a wide step towards creating a life that you desire.
—Brendon Thutso

You are either your own best friend or your own worst enemy
—Brendon Thutso

The ability to embrace and be yourself in a world that is constantly trying to change you is the greatest achievement.
—Brendon Thutso

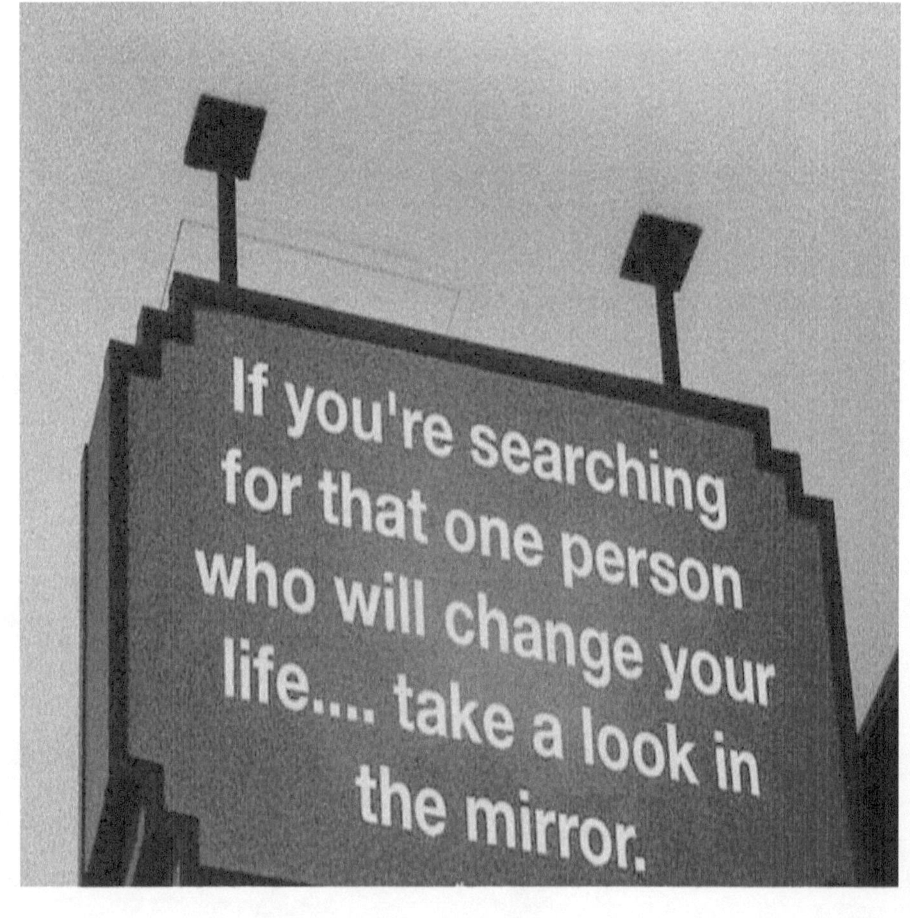

If you're searching
for that one person
who will change your
life.... take a look in
the mirror.